Welcome to xtb Issue Four

Travels Unravelled

XTB stands for **eXplore The Bible**.

Read a bit of the Bible each day.
Zoom in on **Matthew** to investigate the very first Easter.
Wander through the wilderness with the Israelites in **Exodus**.
Join Paul as he travels to Rome in the book of **Acts**.

Are you ready to explore the Bible? Fill in the bookmark...
...then turn over the page to start exploring with XTB!

Table Talk FOR FAMILIES

Look out for **Table Talk** — a book to help children and
adults explore the Bible together. It can used by:

- Families
- One adult with one child
- Children's leaders with their groups
- Any other way you want to try

Table Talk uses the same Bible passages as XTB so that they can be used
together if wanted. Available from your local Christian bookshop or one of our
websites: **UK:** www.thegoodbook.co.uk **N America:** www.thegoodbook.com
Australia: www.thegoodbook.com.au **New Zealand:** www.thegoodbook.co.nz

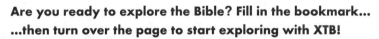

C000162707

Som...... m called

.... (nickname)

My birthday is

....

My age is

....

My favourite place to travel to is

....

OLD TESTAMENT	NEW TESTAMENT
Genesis	**Matthew**
Exodus	Mark
Leviticus	Luke
Numbers	John
Deuteronomy	**Acts**
Joshua	Romans
Judges	1 Corinthians
Ruth	2 Corinthians
1 Samuel	Galatians
2 Samuel	**Ephesians**
1 Kings	**Philippians**
2 Kings	**Colossians**
1 Chronicles	1 Thessalonians
2 Chronicles	2 Thessalonians
Ezra	1 Timothy
Nehemiah	2 Timothy
Esther	Titus
Job	Philemon
Psalms	Hebrews
Proverbs	James
Ecclesiastes	1 Peter
Song of Solomon	2 Peter
Isaiah	1 John
Jeremiah	2 John
Lamentations	3 John
Ezekiel	Jude
Daniel	Revelation
Hosea	
Joel	
Amos	
Obadiah	
Jonah	
Micah	
Nahum	
Habakkuk	
Zephaniah	
Haggai	
Zechariah	
Malachi	

How to find your way around the Bible.

**Look out for the READ sign.
It tells you what Bible bit to read.**

**READ
Acts 23v11**

**So, if the notes say... READ Acts 23v11
...this means chapter 23 and verse 11
...and this is how you find it.**

Use the **Contents** page in your Bible to find where Acts begins

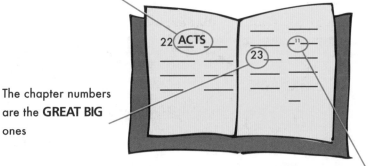

The chapter numbers are the **GREAT BIG** ones

The verse numbers are the tiny **ones!**

**Oops! Keep getting lost?
Cut out this bookmark and use it to keep your place.**

How to use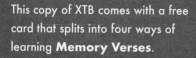

1 Find a time and place when you can read the Bible each day.

2 Get your Bible, a pencil and your XTB notes.

3 Ask God to help you to understand what you read.

4 Read today's XTB page and Bible bit.

5 Pray about what you have read and learned.

6 If you can, talk to an adult or a friend about what you've learned.

YOUR FREE MEMORY VERSE CARD

This copy of XTB comes with a free card that splits into four ways of learning **Memory Verses**.

We'll use it to make a helicopter (that really flies!), a rainbow jigsaw, a hanging globe and a picture frame.

Each one will help you learn a key verse from Exodus, Matthew or Acts.

ACTION STATIONS

The Book of Acts

Acts

Look up **Acts 1v8**

Fill in the gaps in Jesus' words.

"But when the Holy Spirit comes upon you, you will be filled with power, and you will be witnesses for me in

J_____ ,

in all **Judea** and **Samaria**, and to the

e_____ of the earth."

Acts 1v8

Acts

The rest of Acts is the story of 1v8 coming true, as Jesus' followers tell other people all about Him

—first in **Jerusalem**

—then in **Judea** and **Samaria**

—and then further and further and further...

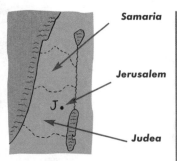

Samaria

Jerusalem

J.

Judea

Acts

Paul's Story

Acts tells us all about Paul. At the start Paul **didn't believe** that Jesus was the Son of God. He **hated** Christians, and did everything he could to have them stopped.

But then Paul himself was stopped—by Jesus! He discovered that Jesus really is **God's Son**, and Paul became a follower of Jesus too. From then on, Paul told everyone he could all about **Jesus**.

Acts

Paul went on **three** long missionary journeys. His **mission** was to tell people about **Jesus**. But Paul made **enemies**. The Jewish leaders **hated** what Paul was **teaching** about Jesus.

Fit the underlined words into the puzzle to find out what happened to Paul.

	E			I		
			E	E		
			E			
	I			I		
E		E		I	E	
	E					

C_____

Paul was arrested and put in chains.

Acts

It looked like the end of the road for Paul. But Jesus had a special message for him.

READ
Acts 23v11

Where had Paul spoken (testified) about Jesus?

In J_____

Where else would he speak about Jesus?

In R_____

The rest of the book of Acts tells us how Jesus' words came true...

Acts

THINK+ PRAY

Jesus promised that the message about Him would spread to "the ends of the earth". His promise came true. The great news about Jesus has spread to **you** and **me** as well!

Thank God that the message about Jesus has spread to you too. Ask Him to help you to learn more about Jesus as you read the book of Acts.

DAY 2 — CHAIN GANG

Paul is in **chains**—but Jesus has promised that he will go to **Rome**, and tell people there about Jesus too.

But first Paul is put on trial, in front of three powerful men. *Take the first letter of each picture to see who they were.*

_____

_____

_____

1. **Felix** was the Roman Governor. He left Paul in prison for two years!

2. He then handed Paul over to **Festus**, the new Governor.

3. Festus didn't know what to do, so he passed Paul on to **King Agrippa**.

Paul told Agrippa how he had become a Christian, a follower of Jesus.

READ
Acts 26v28-32

Fill in the gap (v29).

I pray that you may become what I am —except for these c_____!

Paul wanted all those listening to him to become Christians too.

Did Paul deserve to stay in prison? (v31)   **Yes / No**

Paul had done **nothing** wrong, but he couldn't be set free because he had appealed to have his trial before Caesar, the Roman Emperor.

Now Paul would go to **Rome** —just as Jesus had promised him!

THINK + PRAY

Even when he was chained up in prison, Paul kept on telling people about Jesus.

Are **you** like Paul? Do you tell people about Jesus whenever you can? Do you find that hard or scary? Talk to God about your answers. Ask Him to help you.

STORMY TIMES

Paul was sent by ship to the Emperor in Rome.

The ship left **Caesarea** and sailed up the coast to **Sidon**. Then they headed out to sea, passed to the *north* of **Cyprus**, and arrived in **Myra**. At Myra they changed ships, and set off slowly along the coast to **Cnidus**. Then they crossed over to **Crete**, finally stopping at the safe harbour of **Fair Havens**. (*You can read about this voyage in Acts 27v1-8*)

Draw Paul's route on the map.

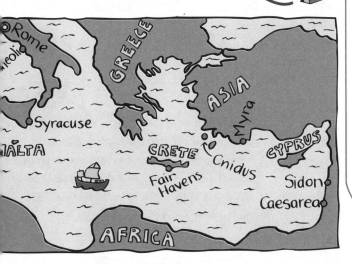

It was a l-o-n-g journey. Over 2000 miles. Normally, sailors didn't sail at this time of year because the weather was far too dangerous. But they decided to go a bit further, to reach a better harbour. It was a **bad decision...**

READ
Acts 27v13-20

The sailors tied down the lifeboat; held the ship together by putting ropes under it; and threw the cargo and ship's equipment overboard.

Find all the red words in the wordsearch. Copy the leftover letter (in order) here.

T_____ G_____ U__ H_____

O	T	H	E	Y
V	T	G	A	V
E	A	E	U	P
R	O	H	O	P
B	B	C	R	E
O	E	A	O	P
A	F	R	P	I
R	I	G	E	H
D	L	O	S	S

PRAY

The sailors could do nothing more to save themselves. So they gave up hope. But **God** was going to save them all (*as we will see tomorrow*). Thank God that we **never** need to give up hope if we have put our trust in Him.

HOPELESS HOPE?

Spot the Difference! *There are eight to find.*

There's no hope!

Don't be afraid!

We saw yesterday that the sailors had given up hope of being saved. But Paul has had a message from God...

READ
Acts 27v21-26

What did the angel say to Paul?

Emperor

afraid

lives

Don't be **a**_____, Paul. You must stand before the **E**_____ .
God has spared the **l**_____ of all who sail with you. (v24)

Did Paul believe God's promises? (v25)

THINK SPOT

The ship was wrecked, and the storm still raging. But Paul had "faith in God that it will happen just as He told me." (v25) Do you think it was easy for Paul to trust God? Why / why not?

Paul told the sailors that he belonged to God and served Him (v23). Over many years, Paul had learned that God **always** keeps His promises. And he knew that God is far more powerful than a storm!

THINK + PRAY

What are some of the things you're afraid of? (*Eg: bullies, being lonely, family problems, war...*) God is **much** more powerful than any of these things! **Ask God** to help you to trust Him to look after you, no matter what you have to go through.

DAY 5 NO WRECKING GOD'S PLANS!

xtb — Acts 27v27-44

The ship has been tossed around by the storm for **two weeks**!
God has promised to **save** everyone on board—but they still have to reach land...

The sailors felt they were close to land – so they checked how deep the sea was.

At first...

It's 120 feet deep.

But then...

Now it's only 90 feet deep!

The sailors let down the lifeboat.

We're going to put out some anchors.

But really they were planning to...

ESCAPE!

Paul knew what was happening.

Unless they stay on board, we can't be saved!

So the soldiers cut the ropes, and set the lifeboat free

Then Paul spoke to everyone.

You haven't eaten for 14 days.

Now eat some food. You need it to survive.

Paul thanked God for the food...

...and they all ate.

You can read this story for yourself in Acts 27v27-37

READ
Acts 27v37-44

What did the ship land on? (v41)
A **sandwich/sandcastle/sandbank**

What did the soldiers try to do? (v42)
Kiss/Kill/Kick the prisoners.

How many people were saved? (v44)
No-one/Someone/Everyone

God kept His promise to save everyone.
Nothing can wreck God's plans!

PRAY **Thank God that He always keeps His promises.**

SNAKES ALIVE!

The ship was wrecked, but the people were all safe. They landed on the island of Malta.

Go back to the map on Day 3. Draw their route from **Crete** to **Malta**.

The local islanders welcomed them warmly. But as Paul collected wood for the fire, something very surprising happened...

READ Acts 28v1-6

When the islanders saw the snake, they thought Paul must be a

m_____ (v4).

How many of the sick islanders were healed? (v9)

Some/None/All

READ Acts 28v7-10

Paul wasn't a murderer or a god! He was a Christian, who served the one true God. So when he found that the chief official's father was ill, Paul **prayed** for him.

But when the snake didn't hurt Paul they changed their minds. Now they thought he was a g_____!

(v6)

THINK SPOT

God had **promised** that Paul would go to Rome, and tell people there about Jesus. So God kept Paul safe on his journey—safe from a shipwreck, and safe from a snakebite.

PRAY

Do you know anyone who travels to tell others about Jesus? (Maybe a missionary, or someone from church?) Ask God to keep them safe as they travel.

DAY 7 ROME AT LAST

↓ ⇧ ↘ △ ⇧

Paul spent three months in _ _ _ _ _ . From

▷ ▽ ◁ ⇧ ⇨ ▽ ▷ ⇩

there he **sailed** to _ _ _ _ _ _ _

◁ ↘ ⇩ ⇦ ↑ ▽ ↓

then further on to _ _ _ _ _ _ and

↖ ▽ △ ⇩ ⬅ ↘ ↑

then _ _ _ _ _ _ _ . From there Paul

◁ ⬅ ↓ ⇩

walked to _ _ _ _ .

Draw Paul's route on the map on Day 3.

Look out for these place names as you read Luke's account of the journey...

READ
Acts 28v11-16

ARROW CODE

⇧ = A
⇨ = C
⇩ = E
⇦ = G
↘ = H
↑ = I
↘ = L
↓ = M
⬅ = O
↖ = P
◁ = R
▷ = S
△ = T
▽ = U
▷ = Y

Paul met up with some Christians in Puteoli. (Your Bible may call them *believers* or *brothers*.) How long did Paul stay with them? (v14) _____

Then some other Christians came from Rome to meet Paul. They came to meet him at the town of Three Taverns (v15)—a walk of over 40 miles!

What did Paul do when he saw them? (v15)
He t_____ **God** and was **encouraged**.

THINK + PRAY

These Christians *encouraged* Paul at the end of his long journey. **Who** do you know who might be sad, ill or lonely? _____

How can you encourage them?

_____

(*Eg: phone or email them, go to see them, or send a card or present.*) Tell them that you are praying for them too.

Ask God to help you to do this.

DAY 8 — THE HOPE OF ISRAEL

Paul had arrived in **Rome**—just as Jesus promised him. But he was also in **chains**, guarded by a Roman soldier. He called the Jewish leaders to see him...

> I did nothing against our people, or our Jewish customs.

> And the Romans found I'd done nothing for which I should die.

> It is because of the hope of Israel that I am bound with this chain.

If you have time, read this story for yourself in Acts 28v17-22

The Jewish leaders wanted to hear more from Paul, so they arranged to come and see him again.

READ
Acts 28v23-24

Fill in the gaps from v23 & v24.

From **m**_____ until evening Paul explained about the Kingdom of

G_____. He tried to convince them about **J**_____ from the Law of

M_____ and the writings of the **P**_____ .

S_____ were convinced. **O**_____ would not believe.

Paul was telling them about "the hope of Israel". Copy the **red letters** (in order) to see what that means.

_ _ _ _ _ _ _ _ _ _ _ _ _ _ _ _ _ _

The hope of Israel (*the Jews*) was that God would keep His promise to send them a new King (called the Christ). Paul used the Old Testament (*the Law of Moses and the Prophets*) to show that **Jesus** was this promised King.

PRAY

Jesus wasn't just "the hope of Israel". He is the hope of the whole world. (*We'll find out more about this on Day 10.*) **Thank God for sending Jesus as our King.**

LOOKING WITHOUT SEEING

Can you read **backwards**? If you're stuck, a mirror will help you.

Isaiah

You will listen and listen, but not understand. You will look and look, but not see.

Isaiah lived more than 700 years before Paul. He spoke these words to the Jewish people of his time.

But now Paul said that they were *also* about the Jewish leaders who were listening to Paul in Rome...

READ
Acts 28v24-28

Fill in the missing words.

The Jews listened l_____ to Paul's words—but they hadn't really heard h_____ him!

Most of them still refused to believe the truth t_____ about Jesus.

But Paul told them that someone else *would* listen to the truth about Jesus. Who? (v28)   The Gentiles

The G_____

People who were not *Jewish* were called *Gentiles*. Paul was saying that they would **listen** to the great news about Jesus, and **believe** it.

THINK SPOT

The great news about Jesus is for **EVERYONE**—for Jews and Gentiles. That includes **you**!

What is your name?

Try writing it in mirror writing!

PRAY

Thank God that the great news about Jesus is for everyone. Pray for anyone who tells you about Jesus. Ask God to help them.

DAY 10 TO BOLDLY TEACH...

xtb Acts 28v30-31

For the next two years, Paul was still in chains, guarded by a Roman soldier. But he lived in his own rented house, and anyone could come to visit him.

READ
Acts 28v30-31

Because he was in chains, Paul wasn't free to **go** where he wanted. But he was free to **say** what he wanted. He carried on teaching boldly.

Who did Paul teach about? **The Lord J_____ C_____**
(v31)

Use the flag code to find out what these names mean.

Jesus means — — —   — — — — —

Christ means

— — — —' — — — — — — —   — — — — —

FLAG CODE

◣ = A
≡ = C
▬ = D
▬ = E
|||| = G
◻ = H
● = I
▮ = K
▦ = N
◥ = O
▭ = S
✕ = V

Turn to **Who is Jesus?** on the next page to find out more. →

Time to think
Paul told everyone he could about Jesus their Rescuer and King.

- Are **you** a follower of Jesus?
- Do you want to be?
  (Go back to **Who is Jesus?** if you're not sure.)
- Do you want to tell your friends about Jesus like Paul did?

PRAY Talk to God about your answers. Ask Him to help you.

WHO IS JESUS?

What does the name Jesus mean?

G _ _ S _ _ _ _

It tells us who Jesus is: He is **G** _ _

It tells us what Jesus does:

He **S** _ _ _ _ _

JESUS IS OUR RESCUER

Jesus has come to save people, as our Rescuer. But what do we need to be rescued from?

Sin

Sin is more than just doing wrong things. We all like to be in charge of our own lives. We do what **we** want instead of what **God** wants. This is called Sin.

Sin gets in the way between us and God. It stops us from knowing Him and stops us from being His friends. The final result of sin is death. You can see why we need to be rescued!

How did Jesus rescue us?
At the first Easter, when Jesus was about 33 years old, He was crucified. He was nailed to a cross and left to die.

As He died, all the sins of the world (all the wrongs people do) were put onto Jesus. He took all of our sin onto Himself, taking the punishment we deserve. He died in our place, as our Rescuer, so that we can be forgiven.

When Jesus died, He dealt with the problem of sin. That means there is **nothing** to separate us from God any more. That's great news for you and me!

Did you know?

Jesus died on the cross as our Rescuer—but He didn't stay dead! After three days, God brought Him back to life! Jesus is still alive today, ruling as our King.

What does the name Christ mean?

G _ _ ' _   C _ _ _ _ _

K _ _ _

JESUS IS OUR KING

Jesus didn't just come as our **Rescuer**. He also came as **King**. Not as a king who lives in a palace, but King of our lives.

We can know Jesus today as our Rescuer, Friend and King—and one day live with Him for ever.

Have YOU been rescued by Jesus? Turn to the next page to find out more...

AM I A CHRISTIAN?

Not sure if you're a Christian? Then check it out below...

> **Christians are people who have been rescued by Jesus and follow Him as King.**

> **You can't become a Christian by trying to be good.**

That's great news, since you can't be totally good all the time!

It's about accepting what Jesus did on the cross to rescue you. To do that, you will need to **ABCD**.

A **Admit** your sin—that you do, say and think wrong things. Tell God you are sorry. Ask Him to forgive you, and to help you to change. There will be some wrong things you have to stop doing.

B **Believe** that Jesus died for you, to take the punishment for your sin; that He came back to life; and that He is still alive today.

C **Consider** the cost of living like God's friend from now on, with Him in charge. It won't be easy. Ask God to help you do this.

D **Do** something about it! In the past you've gone your own way rather than God's way. Will you hand control of your life over to Him from now on? If you're ready to ABCD, then talk to God now. The prayer will help you.

> Dear God,
> I have done and said and thought things that are wrong. I am really sorry. Please forgive me. Thank you for sending Jesus to die for me. From now on, please help me to live as one of Your friends, with You in charge.   Amen

> **Jesus welcomes everyone who comes to Him. If you have put your trust in Him, He has rescued you from your sins and will help you to live for Him. That's great news!**

DAY 11 PAUL'S PRISON POST

Paul was in chains in Rome. But he was free to keep telling people about Jesus. And he was free to write **letters**.

Follow the chains to see three letters Paul wrote from prison.

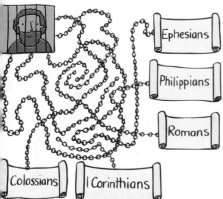

Ephesians

Philippians

Romans

Colossians | Corinthians

Paul wrote **Philippians** to the Christians who lived in the city of Philippi, in northern Greece. In it, Paul told them something very surprising about being in chains...

READ
Philippians 1v12-14

fearlessly
palace
Christ

Wow! Paul said it was a **good thing** that he was in prison! Why?

1 The whole **p**_____ guard knew that Paul was in chains for **C**_____ (v13)

2 Other Christians were encouraged to talk about Jesus **f**_____ (v14)

 THINK SPOT

Paul was stuck in prison. He could have got really cross. Or started sulking! But instead Paul kept talking about Jesus. Every time another soldier was put on guard duty, Paul had someone new to talk with about Jesus. Each guard was a captive audience!

What about **you**? How do you react when things get tough? Do you get cross? Do you start sulking? Or do you ask God to show you ways to keep serving Him?

PRAY

If you want to keep serving God no matter what happens, ask Him to help you. He will!

DAY 12

1 Crack the code to read today's heading.

Paul was in prison, but he still told those reading his letter that they were to rejoice!

READ
Philippians 4v4

If you can, look up "rejoice" in a dictionary. Mine says it means to "feel or show great joy".

2 Who did Paul tell the Philippians to rejoice in?

The L_____

Did you know?

When Paul had visited Philippi himself, he had ended up being whipped and thrown into prison! But he hadn't sat there sulking. Instead, he was **singing**—rejoicing in the Lord!
If you want to know more, and see how God rescued Paul from that prison, read the story in **Acts 16v25-34**

C   E   I
J   O   R

3 MEMORY VERSE CHALLENGE

Make the **helicopter** from your Memory Verse card. While making it, repeat verse 4 to yourself several times until you can remember it. Learn where it comes from too—**Philippians chapter 4 verse 4**

Can you say the verse so quickly that you can finish it before your helicopter lands??

4 Paul didn't just rejoice when things were going well. He even rejoiced in **prison**!

If you are a Christian, there are some great reasons to **rejoice** (even when things seem hard):

PRAY

God loves you.

Jesus wants you to be His friend.

God always listens to your prayers.

Jesus died for you.

Choose some of these to thank God for.

DAY 13 OPEN DOOR

Today's XTB is about opening closed doors. **Close** the door of your room. Sit on the floor, leaning on the door, as you read today's page.

Philippians wasn't the only letter Paul wrote from prison. He also wrote to the Christians in the city of **Colossae** (in modern-day Turkey).

READ
Colossians 4v2-4

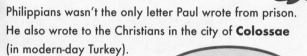

Copy the letters on the **closed** doors to see what Paul was writing about.

P _ _ _ _ _ _

Paul needed God to "open a door". (Some Bibles translate this as "give a good opportunity".) Copy the letters on the **open** doors to see what God needed to open a door for.

The M _ _ _ _ _ _ about Jesus.

Did You Know?

The mystery of Christ (v3) doesn't mean that it's a secret! But we can only know the real truth about Jesus because **God** makes it known to us. If God didn't show us who Jesus really is, it would stay a mystery.

What did Paul ask the Colossians to pray about?

1 That God would o_____ a door, giving Paul opportunities to tell people about Jesus. (*Even in prison!*)

2 That God would help Paul to talk c_____ about Jesus. (v4)

THINK + PRAY

Now **open** the door to your room. Think of somebody you know who tells other people about Jesus. Pray these same two things for them: that God will **open a door** for them to tell people about Jesus; and that He will help them to talk about Jesus **clearly**. Now pray these same two things for yourself as well!

DAY 14 SALT AND...

Salt and Vinegar

Which of these do you like with **salt**?

fish and chips

chicken sandwich

porridge

roast potatoes

popcorn

boiled egg

I put a little salt on all of them—even porridge!

Salt and Prayer

Dear God,
Please open a door—and let me be salty. Amen

Sounds like an odd prayer? It comes from Paul's letter to the Colossians.

READ
Colossians 4v5-6

Salt and Paul

Yesterday we saw that Paul asked the Colossians to pray that God would **open a door**, giving Paul opportunities to talk about Jesus.

Paul also wrote to them about **salt**...

> Let your conversation be always full of **grace**, seasoned with **salt**. (v6)

Did you know?

Grace is the undeserved kindness of God.

God offers us the undeserved gift of forgiveness through Jesus' death for us. So, if our conversation is to be "full of grace", that means full of **Jesus**.

Salt and Your Friends

Salt makes a huge *difference* to food.

Too little makes it dull.

salt mountain
dull chip

Too much can make you sick!

When you chat to your friends, being a Christian should make a *difference* to what you say. You don't want to be like a dull chip! You want to say interesting things about **Jesus**.

PRAY

Do you want to talk to your friends about Jesus? If so, join in with today's prayer: "Dear God, please open a door, and let me be salty. Amen."

Simple Salt Suggestion
Hang a small bag of salt on your bedroom door, to remind you to pray for an open door and salty talk.

DAY 15 SO MUCH MORE...

Can you still remember the Memory Verse from Day 12? Write it here. (*From memory if you can!*)

Rejoice...

When I was a student, I used to help with a Beach Mission in the south of England. The whole team were asked to learn a Memory Verse before they came. It was from another of Paul's prison letters—to the **Ephesians**.

READ
Ephesians 3v20-21

We've already seen that Paul's prison letters encourage us to pray for some BIG things:

- To keep **serving** God, no matter what happens. (*Day 11*)
- To **rejoice** in the Lord, even when things are hard. (*Day 12*)
- To ask God to **open a door** for us to tell people about Jesus. (*Day 13*)
- To ask for help to talk about Jesus in an interesting (**salty!**) way. (*Day 14*)

In Ephesians, Paul gives us the reason why we can be confident when we pray for BIG things like these. *Colour in the **dotted shapes** to see why.*

---

xtb Ephesians 3v20-21

The Beach Mission's aim was to tell people on holiday all about Jesus. That was scary! But our Memory Verse reminded us that **God is able** to answer all our prayers, and to do far more than we could even think of! And He did!

THINK + PRAY

I have a sign above my door. It says, "God is able." It reminds me that God is able to answer all my prayers, and that **nothing** is too hard for Him. God is able to answer all **your** prayers too. Is there anything you are scared, worried, happy or sad about? Talk to God about it now! Then read v20-21 again, and praise God for being so great!

DAY 16 EXTRAORDINARY EXODUS

The first half of **Exodus** shows how God rescued the Israelites from Egypt...

The Israelites had lived in Egypt for 400 years.

God chose Moses to be their leader and rescue them

God had a message for Pharaoh, the king of Egypt.
Let my people go so that they may worship me.

But Pharaoh refused.
I do not know the LORD.
I will not let Israel go!

So God sent ten terrible plagues on Egypt.

After the last plague, (the Passover), Pharaoh let the Israelites go.

Then Pharaoh changed his mind, and chased after them

But God made a dry path through the Red Sea...
...and the Israelites escaped.

They were safe at last!

In the first half of Exodus, we saw the answers to two important questions:

1 Who is King?

Answer : God is the true King

Pharaoh was the powerful king of Egypt. But Exodus shows that **God** is the true King. Nothing and no-one could stop God's plans.

2 What must the Israelites do now that they are rescued?

Answer : Worship God

God is their true King, so it is right to **praise**, **trust** and **obey** Him.

God has done AMAZING things for the Israelites. Will they now praise, trust and obey Him? Time to find out...

More on the next page.

MEMORY OR FORGETORY?

 xtb

I know of an old lady who says that her memory has become her "forgetory". She puts things in it—but then forgets them again!

That was the problem with the Israelites. Their memories quickly became forgetories!

God knew that the Israelites were like this, so He gave them a way of remembering what He had done for them. Each year, they held a festival to remind them of the great way that God had rescued them from Egypt.

All through the Bible, God's people are told to **remember** what He has done for them. But memories too easily become forgetories!

That's what today's Memory Verse is about:

> **Praise the LORD, O my soul, and do not forget how kind He is.** *Psalm 103v2*

Repeat this to yourself a few times until you can remember it. Now find the jigsaw on your Memory Verse card. The words are in the wrong order. Separate the pieces, then put them in the right order. (Try to do it without peeking!)

READ
Exodus 13v8-10

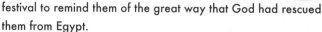

During the festival, they ate bread without yeast (unleavened bread). What did the festival remind them of? (v9)

"The **L**_____ brought you out of **E**_____ by His great power."

THINK + PRAY

Spend a few minutes remembering the great things God has done for **you**. (Think of the good things He has given you, the way He has answered your prayers, and that He sent Jesus to die for you.) Ask God to help you **never** to forget how great He is, or all that He has done for you.

DAY 17 SWEET AND SOUR

Can you remember yesterday's Memory Verse? *Write it here.*

Praise...

The Israelites have safely crossed the Red Sea—just as God had promised. Now they have a choice:

a) **Remember** all that God has done for them, and *trust* and *obey* Him from now on.

b) **Forget** what God has done, and start *grumbling*.

Which do you think they will do?

a) Remember and trust ✔ ✗

b) Forget and grumble ✔ ✗

READ
Exodus 15v22-27

Circle the correct answers.

The Israelites walked **2/3/4** days without finding **milk/cola/water**. When they reached Marah, the water was too **sweet/salty/bitter** to drink. So they **grumbled/trusted God**. God showed Moses some **wood/paper/stone** to throw in the water. This made the water **sweet/salty/bitter**. Then God told them, "If you **ignore/forget/listen to** my commands and obey them, I will not give you the diseases I brought on the **Norwegians/Egyptians/Africans**." Then they came to Elim, where there were **10/11/12** springs of water and 70 **palm/beech/oak** trees.

How were the Israelites to behave if they wanted God to take care of them? (v26)

a) Trust and obey God ✔ ✗

b) Forget Him and grumble ✔ ✗

THINK SPOT

The Israelites needed to be **trusters**, not **grumblers**! What about you? Are you a truster? Or a grumbler?

THINK + PRAY

Make yesterday's jigsaw again. Talk to God as you make it.

Ask Him to help you to be a truster, not a grumbler.

DAY 18   **TRUSTERS OR GRUMBLERS?**

Exodus 16v1-5

XTB Xtra Tough Test

1 What's the second book in the Bible?
a) Genesis   b) Exodus   c) Leviticus

2 What was Moses' brother called?
a) Adam   b) Andrew   c) Aaron

3 How many books in the Bible?
a) 56   b) 66   c) 76

4 How many verses in the Bible?!!
a) 31,202   b) 33,202   c) 35,202

Answers at the bottom of the page.

Yesterday, the Israelites ran out of **water**. They should have *trusted* God, but instead they *grumbled*.
Today, they run out of **food**. Do you think they'll trust God, or grumble?

READ
Exodus 16v1-5

Answers: 1b, 2c, 3b, 4a

Were the Israelites **trusters** or **grumblers**? (v2)

They had been *slaves* in Egypt. It was terrible. But now they'd **forgotten** what it was really like, and **forgotten** all that God had done for them.

God could have been very angry. But instead, He gave them an amazing **promise**!   *Fill in the gaps*

"I will r_____ down food from heaven for you." (v4)

God also gave them a **test**...

"I will t_____ them to find out if they will f_____ my instructions." (v4)

God's Test

The way to show they **trusted** God was by **obeying** God—following His instructions.
(We'll find out if they do follow His instructions in the next few days.)

THINK SPOT

This is true for us too. The way to show that we **trust** God is by **obeying** Him.

Read the words of the prayer below and think carefully about them. Do you want to trust and obey God like this? If you do, say the prayer out loud, and ask God to help you.

PRAY

Father God, thank you for everything You've done for me. Please help me to trust You and to obey You every day, even when that seems difficult or scary. Amen

> In the evening you will know that it was _____ _____ who brought you out of Egypt.

> In the morning you will see the glory of _____ _____.

What do you think the missing words are? *Read the passage to find out.*

READ
Exodus 16v6-8

What were the missing words? **T_____ L_____**
Add them to the speech bubbles above.

God promised to give the Israelites food, so that they will know that He is **their God**, who rescued them from Egypt.

Moses and Aaron called all the Israelites together...

READ
Exodus 16v9-15

God told the **Israelites**, "At twilight you will have **meat** to eat, and in the **morning** you will have all the **bread** you want. Then you will **know** that I am the LORD your God."

What did God send for meat? (v13) **Q_____**
(a bird)

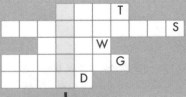

Fit the underlined words into the puzzle to see what God gave them for bread.

M _ _ _ _

"Manna" means "What is it?". The Israelites called this new food *manna* because they didn't know what it was!

Did God keep His promise to give food to the Israelites? **Yes / No**

PRAY **Thank God that He *always* keeps His promises.**

DAY 20   MANNA MANNERS

Follow the instructions to find the mystery object.
Start in the bottom left corner.
Move 3 squares up; then 2 squares right; 3 squares down; 4 squares right; 2 squares up; and 3 squares left.

What did you find? _____

As we saw on Day 18, God gave the Israelites a **test**.

> The people are to go out each day and gather enough for that day. In this way I will **test** them to find out if they will follow my instructions.
> *Exodus 16v4*

God's instructions were very clear. The Israelites were to collect an **omer** of manna each. (An omer is about two litres—the same as a large bottle of cola.) This was just enough manna for one day.

READ
Exodus 16v16-20

The Israelites collected the right amount of manna, just as God said. But what else were they told to do? (v19)

> No-one...
>
>

God had promised to give them food every day. If they **trusted** Him, they didn't need to keep any extra for tomorrow.

But some of the people **didn't** trust God. They kept some manna for the next day. What happened to it? (v20)

It was full of _____

THINK + PRAY

God had done SO MUCH for the Israelites, but some of them still found it hard to trust Him.

Do you find it hard to trust God sometimes? If you do, ask Him to help you to keep trusting Him every day. He will!

DAY 21 **MORE MANNA MANNERS**

Every morning, God gave the Israelites **manna** to eat. He told them to collect just enough for that day. This went on for five days. But on Days Six and Seven the pattern changed. *Crack the code to see the full pattern.*

DAY	How much manna was collected?	Was the previous day's manna fresh?
1 - 5	⬜⬛⬜ Enough for _ _ _ day	⬛⬜ _ _
6	🔵⚫⬜ Enough for _ _ _ days	⬛⬜ _ _
7 (Sabbath)	⬛⬜⬛⬜ _ _ _ _	🔵⬜⬜ _ _ _

⬜ = E
⬛ = N
⬜ = O
⬜ = S
🔵 = T
⚫ = W
🔵 = Y

This was the pattern God gave the Israelites. The seventh day (the Sabbath) was a day of rest. God told them **not** to go and collect manna on the Sabbath—there would be nothing there!

Yesterday, we saw that some of the people **disobeyed** God's instructions. They kept some extra manna, and it ended up full of maggots! How many do you think will keep God's instructions **this time**? **All / Some / None**

READ
Exodus 16v21-30

God had told the Israelites **not** to collect manna on the Sabbath. But how many of them went anyway? (v27)

Have you spotted how the Israelites keep letting God down? He had done SO MUCH for them, but still they didn't trust Him or follow His instructions.

THINK + PRAY

If we're honest, this is what you and I are like sometimes. We don't always trust God, and we don't always follow His instructions. Think carefully about the times when you have let God down. Say sorry to Him for disobeying Him. Ask Him to help you to change.

REMEMBER NOT TO FORGET!

 Exodus 16v31-36

How's your memory?

Tick the ones you never forget.

Your birthday	☐
Your Mum's birthday	☐
Your homework	☐
XTB Memory Verses	☐
(Can you remember both??)	
God loves you loads	☐

Over the last few days, we've seen how the Israelites keep forgetting how great God has been to them. So God tells Moses to do something to remind them in the future.

READ
Exodus 16v31-36

What did manna taste like? (v31)

Moses told Aaron to collect an omer of **manna** (about two litres) and put it in a gold **jar**. They were to keep the jar in a special place, so that all the Israelites could see it for many years to come. It would **remind** them that God gave them food to eat in the **desert** after He rescued them from **Egypt**.

Find the blue words in the wordsearch. Some are backwards!

What do the leftover letters spell?

F _ _ _ _   Y _ _ _ _

 WOW! God gave them enough manna for every day for forty years!

Do you know the Lord's Prayer? Jesus taught it to His followers to show them how to pray. One part of it says:

"Give us today our daily bread."

God doesn't look after us on some days, but then forget us on others! God gives us what we need **every day**. (Just as He gave the Israelites manna for every day.)

PRAY

If you know the Lord's Prayer say it now (or read it from Matthew 6v9-13). Thank God that He loves you **all** the time. Thank Him for giving you what you need every single day.

DAY 23 SPOT THE DIFFERENCE?

Spot the difference. There are eight to find.

The sad thing about this puzzle is that there **should** have been another difference!

No Water—Version One
Back in chapter 15, at *Marah*, the Israelites had no water. They should have **trusted** God, but instead they **grumbled**.

Even though they grumbled, God gave them the water they needed!

This story is in Exodus 15v22-25

No Water—Version Two
In chapter 17, at *Rephidim*, the Israelites again have no water. They should have learned to <u>trust</u> God by now, but instead they still **grumbled**...

READ
Exodus 17v1-7

The Israelites were in trouble—but all they did was *grumble*.
Moses was in trouble too—the people were threatening to stone him to death! Who did Moses ask for help? (v4)

God told Moses to take his staff and hit a rock with it.

Draw what happened. (v6)

PRAY What do **you** do when things are tough? Do you grumble? Or do you ask God for help? Talk to God about your answers.

ARMS FOR THE ARMY

Exodus 17v8-13

XTB Fact File
Four Facts from today's story:

Oops, wrong kind of kite!

1 Amalekites
The Amalekites were a fierce race of people who attacked the Israelites.

2 Joshua
He doesn't know this yet, but Joshua is going to be the next leader of the Israelites. He will go on to lead their army in many battles.

3 Staff of God
This is the staff Moses struck the rock with yesterday, to bring water from it.

4 Praying Hands
Moses prayed with his hands held high.

READ
Exodus 17v8-13

Spot the mistakes in the story below. There are **ten** to find. Circle each one.

The Amalekites came and attacked the Israelites in Manchester. Moses said to Joshua, "Choose some children to go and dance with the Amalekites. I will stand on top of the ladder with the staff of God." As long as Moses held up his feet, the Israelites were winning. But when he lowered his hands, the Eskimos were winning. When Moses' hands grew tired, he sat on a sofa. Aaron and Miriam held his hands up high until morning. So Joshua defeated the Ethiopians.

Prayer made the difference!
Whenever Moses lifted his hands to pray for God's help, the Israelites started to win.

Answers: Manchester, children, dance, ladder, feet, Eskimos, sofa, Miriam, morning, Ethiopians.

Pray like Moses...
Moses trusted God, and prayed. He knew they couldn't win the battle on their own. They needed God's help.

But not exactly like Moses!
In those days people often stood to pray with their hands held up. You can pray like that too if you want—but you don't have to! You can pray sitting, standing, lying down ... at home, at school, outside ... anywhere and anytime.

Prayer Challenge
Find three unusual places to pray today (on a bus? up a tree? in the bath?). Each time, thank God that you can pray anywhere, anytime. Ask Him to help you to trust Him like Moses did.

PRAY

DAY 25 REMEMBER REMEMBER

What will You remember?

Can you remember both Memory Verses? *(They're inside the back cover in case you get stuck.)*

Fill in the gaps below, then cut along the dotted lines. You'll find that yesterday's Prayer Challenge is on the back. Thread your disc onto some wool or string. Hang it somewhere you'll see it every day.

What will They remember?

Look how much God had done for the Israelites:

- Rescued them from **Egypt**.
- Given them **food** and **water** in the desert.
- Saved them from their **enemies**.

But we've seen how quickly they **forget** how great God has been to them. They need help to remember...

READ
Exodus 17v14-16

What did God tell Moses?

Write this down so that it will be
r_____. (v14)

Will they Really remember?

Moses built an altar to God. He called it, "The LORD is my banner." It reminded the Israelites that God was with them, and that He would take care of them and fight for them.

Now the Israelites had a choice:
a) remember: and trust and obey God
b) forget: and disobey God
We'll find out which they do when we come back to Exodus on Day 46.

THINK + PRAY

Read your two Memory Verses again. Spend some time now remembering what God has done for you. Thank and praise Him for all that He has done.

Rejoice in the Lord
a_____. I will say it
again: R_____!
Philippians 4v4

Praise the L_____, O my soul,
and do not f_____
how kind He is.
Psalm 103v2

MATTHEW—THE FINAL PIECE

 **xtb** The Book of Matthew

 I hate sad endings! Do you?

Well, don't worry, because Matthew's book about Jesus has the best ending ever! We're about to look at the last few chapters. But first, check out what's happened so far...

1 The First Christmas

Jesus is born as the promised King.

2 The Last Three Years of Jesus' Life

Matthew tells us all about Jesus' life: about what He did and said.

3 Palm Sunday

At the start of Easter week, Jesus enters Jerusalem on a donkey. The crowds cheer and spread palm branches on the road.

4 The Plot

Not everyone's pleased to see Jesus. The religious leaders hate Him. They plot to have Him killed!

5 Betrayal

Jesus' enemies even persuade one of Jesus' closest friends to help them get rid of Jesus!

Now for the final piece...

Start now on the next page.

xtb Matthew 26v17-19

Have a good look at the picture in the middle. Now cover it up!

What things can you remember from the picture?

1 _____

2 _____

3 _____

Today, Jesus' disciples get ready for a meal. It's a meal to help them **remember**.

READ
Matthew 26v17-19

It's the first day of an important Jewish festival, and the disciples have lots to do!

What's the name of the meal they are preparing for?

The **P**_____
meal.

Find four red vowels hidden in the picture to discover what was remembered at Passover.

R _ S C _ _ FROM _ G Y P T

Jews ate a Passover meal every year to remember that God had rescued them from slavery in Egypt. (*We found out about this meal on Day 16.*)

What an important meal! But something much more important was about to happen!

Find three white consonants in the picture to discover what's about to happen.

JESUS' _ E A _ _

My time has come. (v18)

THINK + PRAY

At your next meal, say thank you to God for everything He has done for you (not just for the food!). Ask God to help you never to forget what He has done for you.

DAY 27 SOME FRIEND

1 Jesus is eating the Passover meal with His friends.

READ
Matthew 26v20-25

What shocking news does Jesus have for the disciples? (v21)

One of you will

_____

2 The religious leaders wanted Jesus dead. **Judas** had already agreed to betray Jesus and hand Him over. But the other disciples didn't know this.

How did the other disciples feel about what Jesus said? (v22)

Draw their faces.

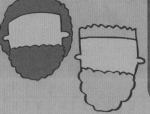

Did you know? "Son of Man" is a title for Jesus.

3 The disciples were sad and shocked.

Is it me?

Jesus knew it was **Judas** who would betray Him (v25), but He didn't try to stop Judas. _Solve the puzzle to find out why._

5 God's	3 part	1 It
2 was	6 plan	4 of

1	2	3
4	5	6

4 Everything was happening just as God planned—just as it says in the Old Testament.

God will punish Judas for betraying Jesus. But God is **so** powerful that the terrible thing Judas did was all part of God's plan!

PRAY **Thank God that He is always in control.**

REMEMBERING RESCUE

Jesus and His disciples are eating the **Passover** meal. They're remembering that **God rescued** the Israelites from **slavery** in **Egypt**.

Find and circle the yellow words in the wordsearch. Some are written backwards!

R	E	V	O	S	S	A	P
J	E	G	Y	P	T	E	S
Y	R	E	V	A	L	S	U
R	E	S	C	U	E	D	S
D	E	G	O	D	A	T	H

From now on, Jesus wants them to remember a different rescue!

READ
Matthew 26v26-30

What did Jesus say about the bread and wine? (v26-27)

This is my
b_____

This is my
b_____

What would the bread and wine remind the disciples of from now on?

Use the leftover letters from the wordsearch (in order).

_ _ _ _ _ _ , _ _ _ _

What did Jesus rescue us from when He died? (v28)

Jesus' blood was poured out for many, for the f_____

of s_____ .

Did You Know?

Sin is doing what **we** want, instead of what **God** wants. Sin separates us from God.

READ verse 28 again.

God promises (makes a covenant) to forgive our sins when we trust in Jesus' rescue on the cross. Jesus rescues us from SIN! That's the rescue to remember! That's why Christians share bread and wine together (sometimes called Communion or the Lord's Supper). It reminds us that Jesus died to forgive our sins.

PRAY
Thank God that Jesus died to rescue you from sin.

DAY 29 TROUBLE AHEAD

xtb — Matthew 26v31-35

Judas is about to betray Jesus and hand Him over to His enemies! How will Jesus' friends react?

READ
Matthew 26v31-35

How loyal will the disciples be to Jesus? (v31)

$$\frac{10}{10} \qquad \frac{5}{10} \qquad \frac{0}{10}$$

Circle your answer

Jesus says they won't be loyal at all. They will desert Him just like it says in the Old Testament. (Like a flock of sheep scattering in panic!)

Who is going to deny Jesus three times? (v34)

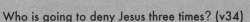

P_____

The disciples don't understand the type of death Jesus must die. Jesus knows that they will be afraid, confused and disappointed. They will run away and pretend they don't know Him.

How loyal do the disciples **think** they are going to be? (v35)

$$\frac{10}{10} \qquad \frac{5}{10} \qquad \frac{0}{10}$$

Circle your answer

They think they know better than Jesus! We'll see...

PRAY It can be hard being Jesus' friend! Ask for God's help.

But there's good news too!
What amazing thing is going to happen? (v32)

Jesus and the disciples will meet in **G_____**

after Jesus has **r_____** from the **d_____**.

DAY 30 NO OTHER WAY

Help! There's someone stuck in the maze! *Find the only way to rescue them.*

READ
Matthew 26v36-46

Choose two words to describe how Jesus is feeling. (v37-38)

_____ and _____

What does Jesus do in these verses?

Underline your answer **Sing** **Sleep** **Pray**

What does Jesus want God His Father to take away? (v39)

> If it's possible, take this c_____ from me.

> *Did you know?*

Jesus knew that on the cross God the Father would punish Him for our sin. He knew it would be like drinking from a cup full of God's anger.

But Jesus wants to do whatever God wants, even if it means facing God's anger! (That's what v42 means.)

Read around the cup to see why it was God's will that Jesus died.

It was the only way to rescue us from sin.

THINK + PRAY

Think how wonderful it is that Jesus was willing to go through so much to rescue you. Thank God for what Jesus did.

Put a ✔ next to the face you think looks most surprised.

Jesus isn't at all surprised by what happens next. See if you are!

READ
Matthew 26v47-56

Who was with Judas? (v47)

A large c_____

Draw some of the things they had with them.

How did Judas let the crowd know which man to arrest? (v48)

✔ your answer

	He gave them a photo.
	He pointed at Him.
	He kissed Him.

The disciples are surprised. They try and defend Jesus with their swords, but Jesus **stops** them.

Why doesn't Jesus resist the crowd? (v54)

	He's too tired.
	He knows He won't win.
	So that everything happens just as the Old Testament says.

What do the disciples do next? (v56)

They scatter like panicking sheep, just as we saw they would on Day 29.

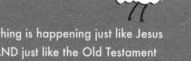

Everything is happening just like Jesus said AND just like the Old Testament writers (prophets) had said. No wonder Jesus isn't surprised!

PRAY **Thank God for His perfect plan to rescue us.**

DAY 32 ON TRIAL

Draw lines to connect the pictures to the right people.

Witness

Judge

Prisoner

I saw him!

Jesus is on trial before the Jewish council (the Sanhedrin).

READ
Matthew 26v57-68

The Judges
What was the council looking for? (v59-60)

Underline the right answers.

False/true evidence so that they could **set Jesus free/put Jesus to death.**

The Witnesses

What were the witnesses like? (v60-61)

☐ Telling the truth clearly

☐ Lying and twisting Jesus' words

Jesus' trial was unfair—but as we'll see later, **He** was still in control!

The Prisoner

Crack the code to see what Jesus says about Himself in verse 64.

I'm the real _ _ _ _ _

D   E   G   J   U

 Matthew 26v57-68

In the Old Testament, Daniel had a vision of a King who would **judge** the whole world and **rule** forever.
Jesus says that's Him!

This is what verse 64 means.

Do the council believe Jesus? (v65-66)

The council think Jesus is speaking *blasphemy* (lying about God). They decide that Jesus should **die**.

The council don't realise it, but it's really **Jesus** who's in control! **He's** the real Judge!

PRAY
Praise God that Jesus is judge and ruler of the world!

attach paper clip here

Day 12 →

*

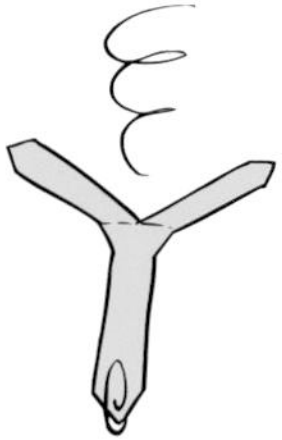

The finished helicopter should look like this... So hold it up high, let it go and watch it fly!

Rejoice in the Lord always. I will say it again: Rejoice!
Philippians 4v4

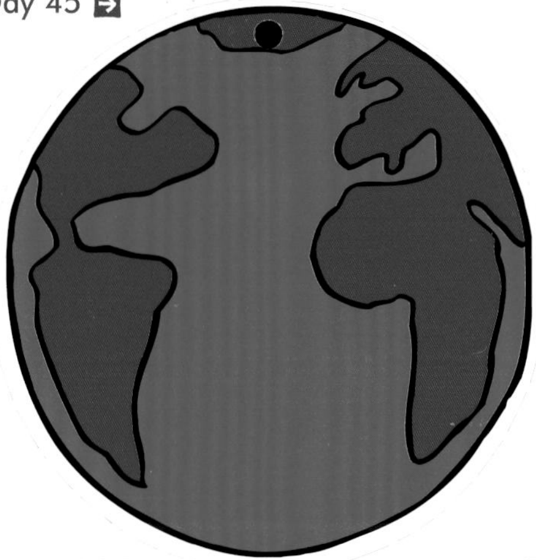

fold along dotted line

punch out along solid lines

separate these two coloured sections

Day 45 →

Day 16 ↓

Day 59 →

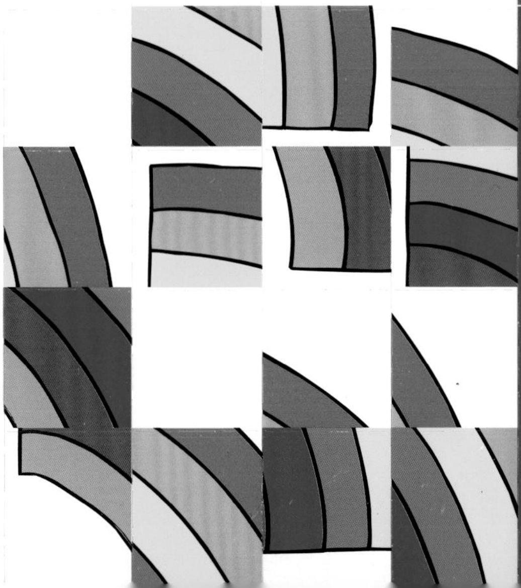

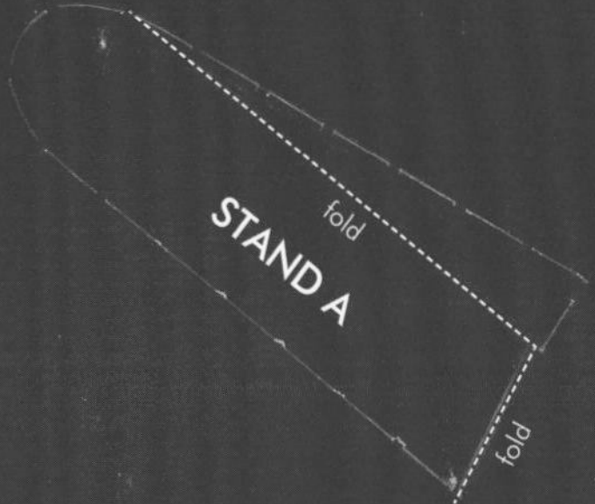

STAND A

fold

fold

fold along dotted line

Love the Lord your God with all your heart and with all your soul and with all your mind. Love your neighbour as yourself.
matthew 27 v 37 & 39

SLOT C

● Go to all
peoples everywhere,
and make them my disciples.
And I will be with you always,
to the end
of the age.

Matthew 28 v 19-20

Picture frame instructions: (You can leave the picture in or
punch it out to make space for your own.) **1.** Punch out
STAND A and fold along the dotted lines. **2.** Fold the whole
frame in half along the dotted line. **3.** Insert TAB B into SLOT C.

These memory verses are designed to
be used with XTB: Travels Unravelled—
Bible-reading notes for children.

Scribbled by Alison Mitchell. Tidied by
Jon Bradley. Pics by Kirsty McAllister.

© The Good Book Company 2003

UK: www.thegoodbook.co.uk
N America: www.thegoodbook.com
Australia: www.thegoodbook.com.au
N Zealand: www.thegoodbook.co.nz

Globe instructions:
1. Punch the main globe shape out. 2. Punch out the
smaller hole at the top. 3. Thread string through the
hole and hang it somewhere you can see it!

✱

Rejoice in the Lord always.
I will say it again: Rejoice!

Philippians 4v4

1. Punch out the whole shape. 2. Separate the two
coloured strips. 3. Fold the coloured strips away from
each other along the dotted line. 4. Attach a paper
clip (not included) to the end marked with a star.

Lord	He	and	Praise
do	*Psalm 103*	O	not
my	the	v 2	how
forget	is.	soul	kind

DAY 33 — NOT ME!

Flashback

> Before the cock crows you will deny me **three** times.

Who is Jesus talking about?

P_____

Peter followed Jesus to His trial and waited outside. Let's see what happens.

One

READ
Matthew 26v69-75

What did the servant girl say to Peter? (v69)

> You were with _____

What did Peter reply? (v70)
Tick the answer.

> Yes, I believe He's God! ☐

> No way! I don't know what you're talking about! ☐

Two

What happened at the courtyard gate? (v71)

_____

What did Peter do this time? (v72)

☐ He was brave and said they were right.

☐ He denied it and swore he didn't know Jesus.

Three

Did Peter deny Jesus a third time? (v73-74)

Shade your answer → **Yes / No**

Whose words did Peter remember when the cock crowed? (v75)

J_____

How did Peter react? (v75)

☐ He didn't care!

☐ He wept and was very sorry.

PRAY

Do you ever pretend you don't know Jesus? Say sorry and ask God to help you tell people that Jesus is your friend.

DAY 34 GUILTY

READ
Matthew 27v1-10

wrong killed 30 innocent

How did Judas react when he heard what had happened to Jesus?

He decided Jesus was **i**_____ and hadn't done anything **w**_____. He returned the _____ silver coins the religious leaders had paid him for betraying Jesus. Then he **k**_____ himself.

Judas told the chief priests that Jesus was **innocent**. Did they care? (v4)

They didn't care at all! They said it was Judas' problem.

But it was **their** problem too! Both Judas AND the chief priests had turned their backs on Jesus. They were both guilty and would be punished by God.

*Solve the puzzle to discover the **only** way to forgiveness.*

Punish yourself ———————————→ FORGIVEN

Believe you're innocent ——————→ STILL GUILTY

Say sorry and ask God for forgiveness ——————→ STILL GUILTY

Sadly, neither Judas nor the chief priests chose the right way.

PRAY Ask God to help you to realise when **you** need to say sorry to Him. Thank Him for sending Jesus as the way to forgiveness.

 The chief priests used the 30 silver coins to buy the potter's field—just as the Old Testament said they would! Everything was happening just as God planned!

PILATE'S PRISONERS

Who should a Judge free? An **innocent** man or a **guilty** one?

READ
Matthew 27v11-19

Pilate had two prisoners. Fill in their names.

J_____ (v11)

B_____ (v16)

 Prisoner One: Jesus

What does Pilate ask Jesus? (v11)

Are you the **K**_____ of the **J**_____ ?

Jesus is **King** of the Jews and of the world, but Jesus knows that Pilate doesn't understand what sort of King!

What does Jesus say to defend Himself? (v12)

ONHTING   **N**_____

 **Wow!** Jesus doesn't defend Himself, or use His power to escape. Instead, He chose to die for us!

How does Pilate's wife describe Jesus? (v19)

Write the **blue** words (*in order*) to see what we know about **Jesus**.

Prisoner Two: Barabbas

Barabbas plotted against the Romans, and he was probably even a murderer.

Write the **red** letters (*in order*) to see what we know about **Barabbas**.

Pilate could only release **one** prisoner. Would it be Jesus or Barabbas? *We'll see tomorrow!*

PRAY But first! Praise Jesus that He never did anything wrong!

Who *deserves* to die on the cross?
Guilty **Barabbas**, or innocent King **Jesus**?

Write their name here. _____

READ
Matthew 27v20-26

Who do the crowds want to set free? (v20-21)

Who persuaded them to choose Barabbas? (v20)

- [ ] a) Barabbas' friends
- [ ] b) The Jewish leaders

What did the crowd say about innocent King Jesus? (v22-23)

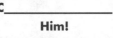
C_____ **Him!**

Pilate knew Jesus was innocent, but he was scared of the crowd and handed Jesus over to be killed.

*Cross out the name Barabbas, and write the name **Jesus** instead.*

Barabbas _____

Jesus took Barabbas' place! Jesus the innocent King was punished *instead of* Barabbas the guilty rebel.

Use a mirror to see who else is a guilty rebel.

We *all* deserve to be punished by God for ignoring Him and doing what we want.

uoY _____

*Cross out the word "You" and write **Jesus** instead, to show that Jesus died to take your punishment.*

PRAY Thank Jesus for taking the punishment for your sin!

DAY 37 MOCK HONOUR

Jesus is **God**, the **King** over all and the great **Rescuer!**

Draw a 😊 in the parts of the shield which describe how we **should** treat Jesus.

READ
Matthew 27v27-36

Shade in the segments that describe how the **soldiers** treated Jesus. ➡

What did they dress Jesus as? (v28-29)
Circle your answer

A soldier

A king

A teacher
ABC

What did they call Jesus? (v29)

Jesus **is** the true King—but they mocked and tortured Him!

(shield diagram with segments: kill, thank, worship, hurt, praise, mock; surrounding letters starting at arrow "start here": K L I A N N G G J O E D S S U R S E I S S C T U H E E P)

Read around the shield to see why God's great King died.

Start at the arrow, and take every second letter.

It was G __ __ ' __

__ __ __ __ __ __ __ __ __

Jesus suffered and was crucified just like God said in the Old Testament. It wasn't an accident. It was the *only* way to rescue us from our sin.

THINK + PRAY

Think of what Jesus suffered for us!

Now look at the segments with a 😊. Ask God to help you to treat Jesus this way.

DAY 38 PROVE IT!

Circle the things you can do.

Ride a bike

Cartwheels

Speak French

Bonjour!

Make a paper aeroplane

Play the recorder

Imagine someone said you **couldn't** do those things!
What would you do?

I'd prove it!
But **Jesus** did something very different!

READ
Matthew 27v37-44

Jesus is dying, but still people go on mocking Him!

How do people want Jesus to prove that He's **God's Son**? (v40)

> Come down from the
> c_____ and
> s_____ yourself!

How do the chief priests want Jesus to prove He's the **King** of Israel? (v42)

> Let him come down from the
> c_____ and we will
> b_____ in him!

They think Jesus has failed. They're sure that God's Son, the King, would never die! They think He's helpless!

What do the chief priests say? (v42)

> He saved others, but he
> c_____ save himself!

 Matthew 27v37-44

Jesus **could** have saved Himself! He **is** God's Son, the King. He could have proved everything, but He had something much more important to do!

Fill in columns 3 and 5 to find out.

1	2	3	4	5	6
	S		V		
U	S		R	M	
			I		

3	5
A	E
F	O
S	N

PRAY Thank God that Jesus didn't save Himself, because He wanted to save us!

DAY 39 ALONE

I hated getting separated from my parents when we went shopping! Has that ever happened to you?

On the cross Jesus was separated from **His** Father.

READ
Matthew 27v45-50

What does Jesus ask God the Father? (v46)

> Why have you _____ me?

God the Father was separated from Jesus for the first time ever, and it was terrible.

What happened to the sky? (v45)

Circle the right picture

Darkness Code

A =

E =

G =

J =

N =

O =

R =

S =

U =

Y =

Use the code to see why God made the sky dark.

To show He was ___ ___ ___ ___ ___

Darkness was a sign of God's judgement.

Who was God punishing? ___ ___ ___ ___ ___

Jesus was separated from God because God was punishing Him! But Jesus had done nothing wrong!

Whose punishment was Jesus taking? ___ ___ ___ ___

Sin separates us from God! On the cross, God punished Jesus for **our** sin. Jesus was separated from God so that **we** don't have to be!

PRAY
Thank God that Jesus was separated from Him so that you don't have to be.

DAY 40 NEW OPENINGS

Draw lines to show what opens these things.

Let's see what Jesus opens!

READ
Matthew 27v50-56

What happened when Jesus died? (v51)

The temple **c**_____ was torn in two.

Unravel the letters in the curtain to see what this means.

    We can be **w**_____ God.

The curtain was there to remind people that sin **separated** them from God. Now it's open!

1 Jesus opened the way for sinners to be with God!

What happened during the earthquake? (v52)

The tombs broke **o**_____.

Unravel the letters in the tomb to see what this tells us. ⟶ We can have eternal **L**_____.

2 Jesus opened the way for people to live forever with God!

What does the Centurion say about Jesus? (v54)

> He really was the **S**_____ of **G**_____.

Wow! An unreligious soldier realises who Jesus is! It's not just Jews who can believe!

3 Jesus opened the way for EVERYONE who believes in Him!

PRAY **Three amazing openings!** Choose one and thank God for it!

DAY 41 DEFINITELY DEAD

 Matthew 27v57-61

Amazing things had been happening! Find these words from yesterday's story in the wordsearch.

curtain   *tombs*   *centurion*   *earthquake*   *bodies*

D	N	O	I	R	U	T	N	E	C
E	C	U	R	T	A	I	N	A	D
E	K	A	U	Q	H	T	R	A	E
T	O	M	B	S	E	I	D	O	B

But Jesus was dead!

READ
Matthew 27v57-61

Who buried Jesus? (v57)

_____ from Aramathea.

Did you know?

Mark's Gospel tells us that Joseph was an important Jewish leader. He had kept his love for Jesus **secret**—but now he wanted to do something for Jesus.

What did Joseph ask Pilate for? (v58)

He asked for _____

Criminals weren't usually allowed a proper burial, but Joseph wrapped Jesus in a clean cloth and gave Him a new tomb.

THINK + PRAY

Joseph showed great love for Jesus. He didn't mind if people found out! Ask God for an opportunity to show people how much **you** love Jesus.

What went in front of the tomb? (v60)

Draw or write your answer.

Two women saw where Jesus was buried (v61). They were both called **M_____**.

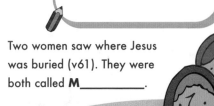

Use the leftover letters from the wordsearch to discover what this passage tells us.

Jesus is definitely __ __ __ __

...but the story isn't over yet!

More tomorrow!

DAY 42 TOMB RAIDERS?

 xtb Matthew 27v62-66

Jesus is definitely dead, but the religious leaders are still worried. They go to see Pilate, the Roman Governor.

READ
Matthew 27v62-66

What do the chief priests and Pharisees remember Jesus saying? (v63)

> After _____ days
> I will rise again.

How do they describe Jesus? (v63)

The _____

Do you think they believe that Jesus will rise from the dead?

No way! They think Jesus was lying. But they're still worried...

What did they think the disciples might do? (v64)

_____ Jesus' body and
_____ people He's alive.

How did they make sure this couldn't happen? (v66)

They _____ the tomb
and _____ guarded it.

Use these words.

tell

steal

soldiers

sealed

No one could steal Jesus' body now!

Jesus said He would rise again after three days.

Finish this sentence using the letters hidden on each soldier (in order).

When Jesus says something will happen

_ _   _ _ _ _ !

PRAY

The Pharisees wouldn't believe what Jesus said. Ask God to help **you** to believe all of Jesus' words.

DAY 43 DEFINITELY ALIVE!

It's three days since Jesus died. The women go to the tomb expecting to find a dead body...

READ
Matthew 28v1-10

What happened when the women arrived?

Underline the correct answers.

There was an **earthquake/volcano** and an **angel/man** rolled the stone away. His appearance was **ordinary/amazing** and the guards **arrested him/became like dead men**.

  I Why wasn't Jesus in the tomb? (v6)

 R He had already ___ ___ ___ ___ ___

There's no body! The tomb's empty! Jesus is alive, just like He said!

 Matthew 28v1-10

Who did the women meet on their way to tell the disciples? (v9)

What did He say? (v10)

Tell my disciples to go to
G_____.
They will **s**_____ me there.

Jesus had promised this before He died. (*It's in Matthew 26v32.*) But how had the disciples treated Jesus since then?

✔ *your answers*

☐ Abandoned Him

☐ Denied Him

☐ Stood by Him

But Jesus still wants to see them! They're forgiven!

PRAY

We treat Jesus badly too. Because Jesus died and rose again, we can say sorry and be forgiven, just like the disciples! Thank God for this!

DAY 44 SPREADING LIES

Matthew 28v11-15

Circle six differences between the soldiers.

READ
Matthew 28v11-15

Who did the soldiers tell about what happened at Jesus' tomb? (v11)

What did the chief priests say to the soldiers? (v12-13)   *Tick your answer*

Jesus must be God. He's alive!

You must lie about what happened!

Underline three differences between these stories.

The disciples opened the tomb. Jesus' body was there. They took it!

An angel opened the tomb. Jesus' body wasn't there. He had risen!

Put a **T** next to the **true** story and an **L** next to the one that is a **lie**.

Which story did the soldiers spread? (v15)

The Truth   **The Lie**

The soldiers were paid to **lie** about Jesus! Tomorrow we'll see how different **we** should be!

It's sad that people believe made up stories instead of the exciting truth that Jesus is alive.

 PRAY

Dear God, help me to believe the truth that Jesus rose from the dead and is alive today!

DAY 45 NEWS FOR ALL

Cross out the **X**, **Y** and **Z**'s to see what Jesus wants.

M Y X O X Z Y R Y E X X D Y I Z Z S Y C I X P Z Y L E Z S

_ _ _ _   _ _ _ _ _ _ _ _ _ _ _

READ
Matthew 28v16-20

What has been given to Jesus by God the Father? (v18)

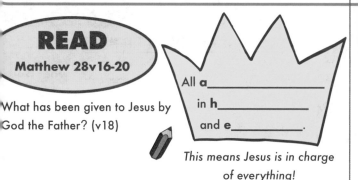

All a_____
in h_____
and e_____.

This means Jesus is in charge of everything!

Who does Jesus want to know about this? (v19)

- ☐ a) The whole world
- ☐ b) A few friends

People **everywhere** need to hear about Jesus because He's the King of the whole world!

xtb   Matthew 28v16-20

Jesus wants people from all nations to become His disciples (followers). *Read around the globe to see what makes a disciple.*

1. Rescued by Jesus. 2. Becomes part of God's family. (Baptism is a sign of this.) 3. Obeys Jesus as King.

What great promise does Jesus give in verse 20?

I am w_____ you always.

Jesus' command is so important I think we should learn it! Find the globe on your Memory Verse card. Repeat the verse a few times to help you learn it—then hang it where you'll see it every day.

THINK + PRAY

Jesus' disciples did what He commanded. (We can read about it in the book of Acts.) Now it's our turn! Who could **you** tell about Jesus? _____ Pray for God's help!

DAY 46 **EXAMINING EXODUS**

The Book of **Exodus** shows us what God is like, and what God's people should be like...

WHAT GOD IS LIKE

He's the __ __ __ __

The first part of Exodus shows us that **God** is the true King. Nothing and no-one (not even Pharaoh, the powerful king of Egypt) can stop God's plans.

He's their __ __ __ __ __ __ __

God **rescued** the Israelites from Egypt, and then kept them safe as they travelled across the desert. As we saw last time, He gave them food and water when needed, and rescued them from the Amalekites too.

Flag Code

B =
C =
E =
G =
I =
K =
M =
N =
O =
R =
S =
T =
U =
Y =

WHAT GOD'S PEOPLE SHOULD BE LIKE

The second half of Exodus shows us what God's rescued people should be like:

__ __ __ __ __ __ __ __ **what God has done.**

__ __ __ __ __ **God for the future.**

__ __ __ __ **God.**

God is their **rescuing King**. Will the Israelites remember what God has done for them, trust Him for the future and obey Him?
It's time to find out...

More on the next page.

DAY 46 ON EAGLES' WINGS
CONTINUED

The Israelites have been travelling in the desert for three months. Now it's time for them to stop...

READ
Exodus 19v1-4

The Israelites camped at the foot of the mountain. *Draw a circle round Mount Sinai on the map.*

God had a message for the Israelites:

> You saw what I did to the
>
> E_____ , and how
>
> I carried you on e_____
>
> wings, and b_____
>
> you here to me. (v4)

eagle's   brought   Egyptians

Like an eagle cares for her young, God had powerfully rescued them from danger, and brought them to be with Him.

God had done **so much** for the Israelites.
• He was their **rescuing King**.
• They were His **rescued people**.
But will they listen to Him now, and obey His words?
We'll find out more tomorrow..

God has done **so much** for us too!
He sent His Son Jesus to die for us, to **rescue us** from our sin.
If we are Christians, then:
• He is our **rescuing King**.
• We are His **rescued people**.

PRAY

As you read through Exodus, you will be reading God's words to **you** too. Ask Him to help you to listen to Him, and to obey His words.

GOD'S CHOSEN PEOPLE

Exodus 19v5-8

God gave Moses a message for His people. Use these words to fill in the gaps. → King Holy agreement God served

READ
Exodus 19v5-8

"If you obey me fully and keep my **covenant**, then you will be my **treasured** possession. The whole earth is mine, but you will be a **kingdom** of **priests** and a **holy** nation." (v5-6)

*Shade in the coins with **X**, **Y** or **Z** on them to see God's special treasure.*

An **a**_____ between God and His people.

G_____ is their true **K**_____.

Priests **s**_____ God and told others about Him. The Israelites were to do this too.

H_____ means "set apart". They were set apart to be *different* from the other nations, because they belonged to God.

How much of God's word did the people say they would obey? (v8)

None / A bit / Most / Everything

THINK + PRAY

Obeying God can be hard. There will be some things you have to stop doing. And you will sometimes have to do things you find scary or difficult. But obeying God is **always** the best for us. Do **you** want to live God's way, as the Israelites said they would? If you do, talk to God about it. Ask Him to help you.

DAY 48 READY FOR GOD

 Exodus 19v9-13

Draw lines linking each object with the thing that cleans it.

Did you know? Newspaper is great for cleaning windows!

The Israelites needed to be **clean**. But not because they were muddy! They needed to be ready for God...

READ
Exodus 19v9-13

Did you know?

The Israelites were told to **consecrate** or **purify** themselves by washing in a special way, so that they were ready to meet God.

GOD IS AWESOME!

He is amazing, powerful and perfect. He is totally pure, and nothing impure can come near Him!

1 *Because God is awesome,* the Israelites must consecrate themselves.

> Moses told them to **w_____** their **c_____** to get ready for God. (v10)

2 *Because God is awesome,* the Israelites mustn't come too close.

> God told **M_____** to set limits to stop the people going up the **m_____**. (v12)

mountain   wash   Moses   clothes

God was going to put on a display of His awesome power. The people would watch... at a distance. Only Moses was allowed to go up the mountain to be with God.

GOD IS AWESOME!

God is still awesome today. We have no right to be near Him. He is too perfect. Too pure. **BUT!**

The great news is that we *can* come to God because of **Jesus**! Jesus died to make a way for us to be with God.

THINK SPOT

Where are you right now?   *at home? holiday?*

PRAY

Thank God that you can talk to Him right now, wherever you are, because of Jesus.

DAY 49 THUNDER STRUCK

Exodus 19v16-25

Choose some words to describe God. (Eg: Loving)

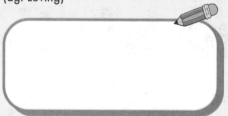

As we read the Bible, we see different parts of God's character. We see that He is loving. He is totally fair. He always keeps His promises. Today, we'll see how **awesome** God is...

READ
Exodus 19v16-19

That morning there was **thunder** and **lightning**, and a very loud **trumpet** blast. Mount Sinai was covered with **smoke**, because God came down on it in **fire**. Then the people felt an **earthquake**. They **trembled** with fear.

*Find the red words in the wordsearch. Look out for **Wow!** too.*

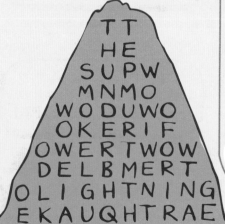

Wow! The people would never forget this day! But God was worried that their curiosity might get the better of them...

READ
Exodus 19v20-25

Moses had already set limits to stop the people going up the mountain.

But God told Moses to warn them again, so that no-one would be hurt.

PRAY

God is awesome! Look back at your list of words at the beginning. Thank and praise God that He is like this.

DAY 50

⑩ ⑤ ④   ⑩ ④ ⑦   ② ⑧ ⑥ ⑥ ① ⑦ ③ ⑥ ④ ⑦ ⑩ ⑨

Exodus 20v1-6

Crack the number code to discover today's title.

On Day 46, we saw what God's rescued people should be like:

- *Remember* what God has done
- *Trust* God for the future
- *Obey* God

Now God is giving them ten laws to obey.

READ
Exodus 20v1-6

What does God remind them? (v2)

> I am the **L**_____ your God, who
> brought you out of **E**_____.

Then He gave them His first two commandments:

| 1 | **No other gods.** |
| 2 | **No idols.** |

A = ①
C = ②
D = ③
E = ④
H = ⑤
M = ⑥
N = ⑦
O = ⑧
S = ⑨
T = ⑩

THINK SPOT

Did you know?

An **idol** is anything we worship instead of God. In Bible times people often made statues to pray to. But an idol today can be anything we treat as being more important than God.

Have a think about what you might be tempted to put first instead of God. The pics and words in the box might help you. Can you add any more?

family · money · schoolwork · popstars · clothes · sport

PRAY

We **all** break these two commandments! None of us always puts God first. Tell God you're sorry for making other things more important than Him. Ask Him to help you to love **Him** more than anything else.

WHAT'S IN A NAME?

Use the Crisscross Code to solve the puzzle.

┐∪∩ ∪⌐⊐⊏∟ ⊐⊐⊏∟

_ _ _ _ _ _ _ _   _ _ _ _

Crisscross Code

C	E	G
I	K	N
R	S	U

G = ∟
S = ∏

Look how much the Israelites already know about God!
He's their **King**. He **rescued** them from Egypt. He is
awesome, **powerful** and **perfect**. Even His **name** is special!

Since God is their rescuing King,
how should they treat Him?

READ
Exodus 20v7

swear   name   joke   wrong

Fill in the gaps to see what this means.

It means never
J _____
about God.

And don't use God's
n _____ (or Jesus)
as a **s** _____ word.

And don't think
w _____
things about God.

THINK SPOT

How do you feel when you
hear people swearing?
Imagine what it would be like
if people used **your** name as
a swear word! How would
it make you feel?

God always hears us if
we say or think wrong things about Him!
Imagine how it makes Him feel.

THINK + PRAY

Do you ever use God's
name as a swear word?
Or think wrong things
about God? If you do,
tell Him you are sorry,
and ask Him to help you
to change.

DAY 52 REST IS BEST

Imagine going to school on Monday and Tuesday and Wednesday and Thursday and Friday and Saturday and Sunday and Monday and Tuesday and...

Imagine never getting a day off!

How would you feel?

The fourth commandment is about having a rest.

READ
Exodus 20v8-11

God made our world, and then rested (v11). In the same way, the Israelites were to work for six days, and then have a day of rest.

Some Bible versions list "aliens" in v10, but they're not little green men! It means foreigners who live with the Israelites. The rest day is for them too.

The Israelites were told not to do any **work** on the Sabbath.

Do you remember that they collected twice as much manna the day before, so that they could rest on the Sabbath?

(We read about this on Day 21.)

But a day of rest doesn't mean spending all day sleeping!

Fill in the missing vowels (a e i o u).
It's a great day to
m__ __t with other Chr__stians, to learn t__gether about J__s__s.
It's also a great day to
d__ s__meth__ng you __nj__y.

What do you enjoy doing, that you could do on your rest day?

What can YOU do to make one day special?

Go for a walk or bike ride, and thank God for our wonderful world.

If you enjoy reading, read a book. If you enjoy roller blading, take your blades to the park.

Make sure you've already finished any homework, so you don't have to do it on your rest day.

Go to church or a Christian group to learn together about Jesus.

PRAY
Ask God to help you make one day special.

DAY 53 MUMS AND DADS

Spot eight differences.

Is this what it means to "honour" your parents? Let's find out.

READ
Exodus 20v12

Do you honour (respect) your parents or guardians?
Look at the list below, and mark yourself **honestly**!

	Rarely	Sometimes	Always
Obey them			
Be polite to them			
Help them			
Listen to them (without interrupting)			
Thank them			

xtb — Exodus 20v12

How do you react when you're asked to do something?

a) Complain
b) Hide
c) Put it off
d) Obey straight away

There's a really good reason why we should always give answer d). To find it, copy the red letters into the gaps below.

"Children, obey your parents in everything, for this

_ _ _ _ _ _ _ _   _ _ _   _ _ _ _."

Colossians 3v20

Do you want to **please God** by honouring your parents?
Here are some ways you can do that:

Do what they say without grumbling.

Tell them you love them.

Only say good things about them to others

Thank them for taking care of you.

Help at home without being asked.

PRAY

Choose one (or more!) of these and do it today.
Ask God to help you.

We're zooming through the ten commandments. Today we've reached Number Six.

Can you read backwards? If not, use a mirror.

Do not murder.
Exodus 20v13

Hmm. That sounds OK, doesn't it? I'm sure you've never murdered anyone! Neither have I.

But let's check out what **Jesus** said about it...

READ
Matthew 5v21-22

You and I were made by God—and He loves us. That's great isn't it? But He also made and loves everyone else in the world. And that makes a difference to how we treat them.

way   *life*   *God*   *take*

G_____ chose to give each person l_____.
So it's wrong to t_____ their life
a_____ by murdering them.

---

xtb   Matthew 5v21-22

But Jesus said this commandment is about more than murder.

Who did He say it's about? (v22)

Anyone who is a_____ with his brother...

*This means **everyone**, not just your little bro!*

hate   *names*   *fight*   *loves*

God made and l_____ each person.
So it's wrong to h_____ them, f_____
with them or call them n_____.

God is a God of love. So WE should be loving too.

THINK + PRAY

Is there anyone you find it really hard to like? Do you ever tease people? Or call them names? Ask God to help you to change, and to treat people the way He wants you to.

FAMILY MATTERS

xtb Exodus 20v14

Spot eight differences.

They look like a perfect, happy family. But families aren't always happy, are they?

READ
Exodus 20v14

God invented marriage.
God said that marriage should be for life. So this seventh commandment says that you mustn't take someone else's husband or wife (adultery).

Families matter to God.
This commandment protects families from being broken up.

Think about your family.

Draw them here, or write their names.

FAMILY PRAYERS

* Thank God for each person in your family.

* Is anyone in your family sad, worried or ill? Pray for them. Ask God to help them.

* Have you done anything special together as a family, or are you planning to? Thank God for special times together.

* Is there anything about your family that makes you sad? Talk to God about it. (*You may want to talk to an older Christian about it too.*)

* Ask God to help you to love each person in your family, and to find ways to show them that you love them.

THINK + PRAY

DO NOT _ _ _ _ _ _

Exodus 20v15

Read the verse, then fill in the missing word in today's title.

READ
Exodus 20v15

Copy the blue letters here.

Copy the red letters here.

G _ _ _ _ _ _ _ _
_ _ _ _ _ _ _ _

The Bible tells us that **God** gives us everything that we have. He gives us good gifts.

If we steal, it's like telling God, "You haven't given me enough. I need more!"

It shows that we don't trust God to give us everything we need.

G _ _ _ _ _ _
_ _ _ _ _ _ _ _

People matter to **God**. He made and loves them. We should treat other people the way God wants us to.

If we steal from people, we hurt them.
It shows that we don't love them the way God wants.

Have you ever...
a) shoplifted?
b) borrowed something and not returned it?
c) taken stuff you weren't supposed to?
d) dodged a bus fare?

If we do any of these things we cheat and hurt others—AND GOD!

If you have stolen anything, say **sorry** to God. Ask Him to help you to change.

PRAY

Thank God for the good things He has given you. Ask Him to help you to trust Him for everything you need.

DAY 57 LIE HEARTED

What is **God** like? (Circle) your answer
Unloving/Slightly loving/Totally loving

What are **God's words** like?
Always true/Sometimes true/Never true

Now see what God wants **us** to be like.

READ
Exodus 20v16

Did You Know?

Giving **false testimony** means lying about someone. Like the false witnesses who told lies about Jesus at His trial. (Matthew 26v59-61)

I hate Joel! Let's say that he stole two of your sheep.

Good idea. That'll get rid of him!

Why is this wrong? *Tick your answers*

a) God's 9th commandment forbids it.
b) Joel would be punished for something he hadn't done.
c) God's people should only speak the truth—just as God does.
d) God's people should love each other—just as God loves them.

Which ones did you tick? _____

All of these answers are true. The ten commandments showed God's rescued people how to live. They were to be like Him, and show others what He is like. God is *loving* and *truthful*. They should be too.

I can't stand Lisa! Let's tell Mr Harris she nicked your new pens.

Yeah, great! That'll sort her!

Why is this wrong? *Explain it in you own words*

PRAY

Say sorry to God for any times you have lied about someone else. Thank God that **His** words are always true. Ask Him to help **you** to be truthful too.

IT'S NOT FAIR!

Look at that! Jon's got a new skateboard!

Wow! Those new ones cost a bomb!

And a miniature TV!

And Jen told me he's got his own DVD in his room.

Huh! I never get great stuff like that.

It's not fair!

Do you ever feel like this? Let's see what the last commandment says about it.

READ
Exodus 20v17

Did You Know?

Covet/Desire—means longing to have something that someone else has.

Circle the things the Israelites were told not to covet (desire).

If you're like me, you've probably never wanted someone else's ox! But look at the picture again. Underline anything **you** might get jealous about.

God doesn't really love me. He hasn't give me enough. I want more!

I'm sure you wouldn't say anything like that! Would you???

BUT if we are jealous of what other people have, this **is** what we are saying to God! We're saying that He hasn't given us enough.

THINK+PRAY

Have you ever **coveted** something that wasn't yours? Clothes? Friends? Money? If you have, say sorry to God and ask Him to help you not to get jealous.

Ask God to help you to trust **Him** to give you everything you need.

The Ten Commandments

1 No other gods
2 No idols
3 Don't misuse God's name
4 Keep one day special
5 Honour your parents

6 Do not murder
7 Don't commit adultery
8 Do not steal
9 Don't lie about others
10 Don't be jealous of others

Which commandment is the greatest?

How would you answer Tom's question?

Some of Jesus' enemies (religious leaders called Pharisees and Sadducees) asked Jesus the same question. Let's see what He said...

READ
Matthew 22v34-40

Fill in the gaps.

Love the Lord your **G**_____ with all your _____, with all your _____ and with all your _____. (v37)

This means loving God **totally**, with every part of you.

Love your _____ as you love _____.

This means loving **everyone**, not just neighbours!.

What a fantastic answer! *Crack the code to see why.*

A	D	G	L	O	S	W
⇧	⬊	⇦	⬋	⬅	▷	◁

This sums up all of

⇦ ⬅ ⬊ ▷ ⬋ ⇧ ◁

'
— — —   — — — —

That's what verse 40 means.

Look again at the ten commandments.
—which ones are about **loving God**?
—which ones are about **loving other people**?

You will find Jesus' summary on your Memory Verse card. Follow the directions to make a picture frame. Put a photo, magazine pic or drawing inside it. Put it somewhere you'll see it every day.

THINK+PRAY

Jesus' words mean that we must love God totally, and love other people just as much as we love ourselves. That's really hard to do! We need God's help. Ask God to help you to love Him and other people more and more.

WE WILL...

 Exodus 24v3-8

As well as the ten commandments, God gave Moses many other instructions about how the Israelites were to live. (They're in chapters 20-23.) We're going to jump ahead to see how the Israelites responded.

Crack the code to see *what they said.*

G	H	I	N	R	T	V	Y
⇦	↖	↑	↙	▽	△	◁	☀

We will do

⇩ △ ⇩ ▽ ☀ ◁ ↖ ↑ ↙ ⇦

___ ___ ___ ___ ___ ___ ___ ___ ___ ___

the Lord has said.

What a **H-U-G-E** promise to make to God!

READ
Exodus 24v3-8

Moses wrote down **everything** God had said. In the morning, Moses built an **altar**—a stone table where God's people cooked special **animals** and gave them as a **gift** (sacrifice) to God. Moses read God's laws to the people, and they promised to **obey** them all. Then Moses took some of the **blood** from the **sacrifices**, and **sprinkled** it on the people.

Fit all of the underlined words into the puzzle below to discover a hidden word.

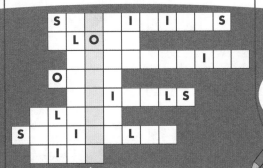

A **covenant** is a special agreement that mustn't be broken. This covenant was between God and His people. God **always** kept His part of the covenant. He took care of the Israelites, and kept all of His promises to them.

The Israelites had just promised to obey everything God had said. Do you think they will keep their promise? (We'll find out tomorrow...)

PRAY

All the way through the Bible we see that God is a **Promise-Giver** and a **Promise-Keeper**. God never makes promises that He can't keep! Thank Him for being like this.

DAY 61 CALF HEARTED

The Israelites had just promised to keep all of God's laws. But while Moses was up Mount Sinai, they got restless...

Moses was on Mount Sinai with God. He was there for 40 days and nights.

So the Israelites went to Aaron, Moses' brother.
We don't know what's happened to Moses.

Make gods for us, to lead us.

Aaron agreed.
Bring me all your gold earrings

So the people brought their earrings to Aaron.

And Aaron made them into a statue of a golden calf.

The people worshipped the statue.
These are our gods, who led us out of Egypt!

Then they held a festival to celebrate.

READ
Exodus 32v1-6

Cross out the **X**s.

Yesterday, we saw that the Israelites promised to **XOXXBXEXXYX** everything God had said to them.

But 40 days later they **XFXXORXGXXOXTX** their promise, and **XTXURXXNXEXDX XAXXWXAXXYX** from God!

Are you shocked by what the Israelites did? As we read about the Israelites in Exodus we often see them forget what God has done for them, and stop trusting Him. Sadly, **we** are like this too. All of us easily forget God and turn away from Him.

PRAY

Dear God, I'm sorry for the times when I've turned away from You. Please help me never to forget all that you've done for me. Please help me to keep trusting You, no matter how hard that is. Amen

STIFF-NECKED PEOPLE

Follow the lines to see where the donkey ends up.

green field

muddy hole

sandy beach

warm stable

The Israelites were like this muddy donkey! God had shown them the **best way** to live. But like stubborn donkeys they refused—and went their **own way** instead. So God called them **stiff-necked!** A stubborn people.

READ
Exodus 32v7-10

The people had forgotten their promise to God, and turned their backs on Him. God was right to be angry. They had **sinned**.

But look what Moses said...

READ
Exodus 32v11-14

Fill in the gaps

promises   mountains   Abraham   Egyptians   kill

Why should the **E**_____ say, "He brought them out of Egypt to **k**_____ them in the **m**_____." (v12)

Remember the **p**_____ you made to **A**_____, Isaac and Jacob. (v13)

Did God destroy the Israelites? (v14)   **Yes/No**

The Israelites had **sinned**. They **deserved** to die. But instead God showed them **mercy**—that means **undeserved** kindness.

We'll find out more about sin, anger and mercy tomorrow.

PRAY   Thank God that He is merciful—showing loving kindness to all His people (including you and me!) when we don't deserve it.

DAY 63 ANGER AND MERCY

xtb
Exodus
32v15-20

We saw yesterday that God was **angry** with the Israelites. When Moses came down the mountain and saw the golden calf, **he** was angry too.

READ
Exodus 32v15-20

Moses was carrying two stone tablets with the ten commandments written on them. What did he do with them? (v19)

Write or draw your answer

What did Moses do with the golden calf? (v20)

mixed   ground   burned   drink

- **b**_____ it in the fire;
- **g**_____ it to powder;
- **m**_____ it with water;
- and made the Israelites **d**_____ it!

THINK SPOT

The Israelites had **sinned**. And sin must always be punished. Some of them died because of what they had done, and others became ill. (This is in v25-35.)

God could not let their sin go unpunished.

That's true for us too. We all sin— and sin **must** be punished.

But the great news is that someone came to take the punishment in our place! Who? **J**_____

*Turn to **"Who is Jesus?"** opposite Day 10 to find out more.*

THINK + PRAY

Sin must always be punished. But God showed us great **mercy** (undeserved kindness) by sending Jesus to die in our place, and take the punishment we deserve.

Thank God for loving you so much that He sent His own Son, Jesus, to die for you.

STILL STIFF-NECKED

xtb Exodus 33v1-17

God's mercy is amazing! The Israelites had sinned against Him—worshipping a golden calf instead.

READ
Exodus 33v1-3

Wow! God is still keeping His promise to give the Israelites a land of their own (Canaan) to live in.

But! What did God say?

Moses needed God to go with them. He would rather stay where they were in the desert than go without God!

What was God's answer? (v14+17)

God promised to

____ ___ _____ ____ ___ ___ ___

But God **didn't**

_ _ _ _ _ _ _ _ _ them.

(As we saw on Day 62.)

Take the first letter of each picture

I will **n_____** go with you, because you are a stiff-necked people and I might **d_____** you on the way. (v3)

The Israelites haven't changed. They are still stiff-necked, stubborn people, who will turn away from God again.

But Moses knew that they **needed** God to go with them. In a special meeting tent, He pleaded with God...

But God now gives them a

_ _ _ _ _ _

READ
Exodus 33v12-17

THINK + PRAY

The Israelites are still stubborn sinners. They don't deserve to be given the promised land, or for God to go with them. But God gives them these amazing promises—because God is so loving and merciful. **Thank God for being like this.**

DAY 65 GOD'S GLORY

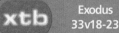
Look what God has given the Israelites:

- God has given them **His law**, to show them how to live.
- He has promised to give them a **land** of their own to live in.
- He has promised to **go with them**.

But now Moses asks God for one more thing.

Show me your _ _ _ _ _

READ
Exodus 33v18-23

A	C	D	E	G	I	L

M N O P R S Y

God warned Moses that he couldn't **see** God's face. But he was allowed to see just a *little* of what God is like.

And he **heard** what God is like too!

What did Moses discover about God?

God is _ _ _ _ _

God shows _ _ _ _ _

And _ _ _ _ _ _ _ _ _ _ _

Did you know?

Mercy means showing incredible kindness to someone who doesn't deserve it.
Compassion means caring for people in trouble.

The rest of Exodus (and the rest of the Old Testament as well!) shows how our **good** God continued to show **mercy** and **compassion** to the Israelites. Even when they sinned against Him, God kept **all** of His promises to them.

THINK SPOT

Are **you** like Moses? Do you want to know God better, and discover more about Him?

Like Moses, we can't see God's face yet. Not until we live with Him for ever in heaven!

But we **can** get to know God better, by reading His book, the Bible.

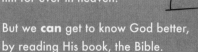

PRAY

Father God, thankyou for the Bible. Please help me to get to know You better and better as I read it. Amen

TIME FOR MORE?

Have you read all 65 days of XTB?
Well done if you have!

How often do you use XTB?
- Every day?
- Nearly every day?
- Two or three times a week?
- Now and then?

XTB comes out every three months. If you've been using it every day, or nearly every day, that's great! You may still have a few weeks to wait before you get the next issue of XTB. But don't worry!—that's what the extra readings are for...

XTB TIME

When do you read XTB?

In the morning.

When I get back from school.

At bedtime.

EXTRA READINGS

The next four pages contain some extra Bible readings about Jesus. If you read one each day, they will take you 26 days. Or you may want to read two or three each day. Or just pick a few to try. Whichever suits you best.
There's a cracking wordsearch to solve too...

The extra readings start on the next page

TIME TO REMEMBER...

Hopefully you have learned four memory verses as you've read this issue of XTB. These extra readings would all make great memory verses too. They're all about **Jesus**—about why He came, and how we can follow Him. Choose one or two to learn as you read them.

The ideas in the box will help you...

PRAY	Ask God to help you to understand what you read.
READ	Read the Bible verses, and fill in the missing word in the puzzle.
THINK	Think about what you have just read. Try to work out one main thing the writer is saying.
PRAY	Thank God for what you have learned about Him.

There are 26 Bible readings on the next three pages. Part of each reading has been printed for you—but with a word missing. Fill in the missing words as you read the verses. Then see if you can find them all in the wordsearch below. Some are written backwards—or diagonally!

If you get stuck, check the answers at the end of Reading 26.

F	A	T	H	E	R	E	S	H	E	P	H	E	R	D
I	R	H	E	W	A	Y	W	A	Y	O	U	T	E	O
N	S	I	R	E	I	G	O	O	D	O	K	O	T	G
V	A	S	E	N	S	E	R	P	R	A	Y	D	U	E
I	V	E	S	N	E	E	D	E	E	R	O	A	R	R
S	I	V	A	N	D	T	A	B	L	E	Y	Y	N	U
I	O	O	Y	O	U	S	L	U	F	K	N	A	H	T
B	U	L	O	S	T	T	A	L	K	J	X	T	B	P
L	R	E	J	O	I	C	E	L	O	K	E	Y	Y	I
E	X	T	B	R	A	C	E	A	B	L	E	S	O	R
D	E	A	T	H	C	A	L	M	S	A	F	E	U	C
B	E	L	I	E	V	E	S	B	T	I	R	I	P	S

Memory Verses about Jesus

Tick the box when you have read the verses.

☐ **Read Hebrews 13v8**

...us never changes. Everything we ...d about Him in these extra readings ... be true for ever.

...sus Christ is the same yesterday, **t** _ _ _ _ and forever." (v8)

☐ **Read John 14v6**

...us is the only way to ...w God.

...us said, "I am the **_ _ _** , the truth and ... life; no one goes to the ...her except by me." (v6)

☐ **Read John 1v29**

...us died to take the punishment for ... sin.

...here is the **L** _ _ _ of God, who ...es away the sin of the world!" (v29)

---

4 ☐ **Read Acts 2v24**

Jesus rose again from the dead. He is still alive today!

"But God raised Him from **d** _ _ _ _ setting Him free from its power, because it was impossible that death should hold Him prisoner." (v24)

5 ☐ **Read John 10v14-15**

Jesus described Himself as our good shepherd, who dies for His sheep.

"I am the good **S** _ _ _ _ _ _ _ ." (v14)

6 ☐ **Read Colossians 1v15**

Jesus shows us what God is like.

"Christ is the visible likeness of the **i** _ _ _ _ _ _ _ _ _ God. He is the firstborn over all creation." (v15)

Memory Verses about why Jesus came

7 ☐ **Read Matthew 1v21**

An angel told Joseph that Jesus was coming to save us.

"She will have a son, and you will name him **J** _ _ _ _ —because he will save his people from their sins." (v21)

8 ☐ **Read Luke 2v11-14**

The angels told the shepherds that Jesus, their Rescuer, had been born.

"This very day in David's town your **S** _ _ _ _ _ _ was born—Christ the Lord!" (v11)

9 ☐ **Read John 3v16**

The most famous verse in the Bible!

"For God loved the world so much that He gave His only Son, so that everyone who **b** _ _ _ _ _ _ _ in Him may not die but have eternal life." (v16)

10 ☐ **Read Luke 19v10**

Jesus (sometimes called The Son of Man) came to rescue us.

"The Son of Man came to seek and to save the **l _ _ _** ." (v10)

11 ☐ **Read 1 John 4v10**

Why did God send Jesus?—because of His everlasting love for us.

"This is what **l _ _ _** is: it is not that we have loved God, but that He loved us and sent His Son to be the means by which our sins are forgiven." (v10)

12 ☐ **Read Romans 4v25**

Jesus died for our sins—but He didn't stay dead! God brought Him back to life.

"Because of our sins He was handed over to die, and He was **r _ _ _ _ _** to life in order to put us right with God." (v25)

Memory Verses about following Jesus

13 ☐ **Read John 15v12**

We are to love each other, just as Jesus loved us.

"My commandment is this: love one another, just as I love **y _ _** ." (v12)

14 ☐ **Read John 15v14**

If we are Jesus' friends, we will want to obey Him.

"You are my **f _ _ _ _ _ _** if you do what I command you." (v14)

15 ☐ **Read Galatians 5v22-23**

The Holy Spirit changes us to become more like Jesus.

"But the **S _ _ _ _ _** produces love, joy, peace, patience, kindness, goodness, faithfulness, humility and self-control." (v22-23)

16 ☐ **Read Philippians 4v4**

Christians aren't always happy. But th have a deep down joy because Jesus their Rescuer and King.

"Rejoice in the Lord always. I will say again: **R _ _ _ _ _ _** !" (v4)

17 ☐ **Read Hebrews 12v1-2**

Like an athlete, we must keep going, and never give up.

"Let us run with determination the **r _ _ _** that lies before us." (v1)

18 ☐ **Read 1 Corinthians 10v13**

Sometimes we will be tempted to do wrong things. But God promises to giv us a way out.

"God will not let you be tempted beyond what you can bear. But when you are tempted, He will also provide **W _ _ O _ _** so that you can stand up under it." (v13)

Read Romans 8v15-16

...e are followers of Jesus, we can call
...d our Father.

...e Spirit makes you God's children,
...d by Him we cry out to God, 'Abba,
... _ _ _ _ _ .' " (v15)

Read Romans 8v28

...d is always in control. His good
...poses always work out.
...e know that in all things God works
g _ _ _ with those who love
...n, those whom He has called
...ording to His purpose." (v28)

Read Ephesians 3v20-21

...d is able to do far more than we can
...r imagine!
...o Him who by means of His power
...rking in us is **a** _ _ _ to do so
...ch more than we can ever ask for, or
...n think of: to God be the glory in the
...rch and in Christ Jesus for all time,
...ever and ever! Amen." (v20-21)

Memory Verses about Prayer and the Bible

22 ☐ **Read Matthew 6v9-13**

*Jesus taught His followers how to pray.
(This is often called The Lord's Prayer.)*
"This, then, is how you should
p _ _ _:
Our Father in heaven..." (v9)

23 ☐ **Read 1 Thessalonians 5v16-18**

*We can pray to God anywhere, any
time. There's loads to thank Him for,
even when things seem hard.*
"Be joyful always, pray at all times, be
t _ _ _ _ _ _ _ in all
circumstances." (v16-18)

24 ☐ **Read Philippians 4v6-7**

*We can pray about everything. We
don't need to worry.*
"Don't **w** _ _ _ _ about anything,
but in all your prayers ask God for what
you need, always asking Him with a
thankful heart." (v6)

25 ☐ **Read 2 Timothy 3v16-17**

*The Bible is God's word to us. It shows
us how to serve Him.*
"All **S** _ _ _ _ _ _ _ _ _ is
inspired by God." (v16)

26 ☐ **Read
Hebrews 4v12**

*The Bible shows us when we're not
following Jesus too. It helps us to
change.*
"The word of God is alive and active,
sharper than any double-edged
s _ _ _ _ ." (v12)

WHAT NEXT?

XTB comes out every three months. Each issue contains 65 full XTB pages, plus 26 days of extra readings. By the time you've used them all, the next issue of XTB will be available.

ISSUE FIVE: The Promise Keeper

Issue Five of XTB explores the books of Mark, Numbers, Deuteronomy and Ephesians.

- Investigate who Jesus is and why He came in **Mark's** Gospel.
- Continue journeying with the Israelites in **Numbers** and **Deuteronomy**.
- Read one of Paul's prison letters—to the **Ephesians**.

Available from your local Good Book Company website:

UK: www.thegoodbook.co.uk
N America: www.thegoodbook.com
Australia: www.thegoodbook.com.au
N Zealand: www.thegoodbook.co.nz

XTB Code Crackers

Use these codes to crack the Memory Verses opposite.

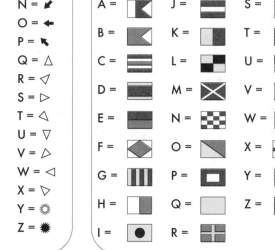

ARROW CODE

A = ⇧   N = ↙
B = ⬈   O = ←
C = ⇨   P = ↖
D = ⬃   Q = △
E = ⇩   R = ◁
F = ⬂   S = ▷
G = ⇦   T = ◁
H = ⬅   U = ▽
I = ↑   V = △
J = ↗   W = ◁
K = →   X = ▽
L = ↘   Y = ☀
M = ↓   Z = ✷

FLAG CODE

A =   J =   S =
B =   K =   T =
C =   L =   U =
D =   M =   V =
E =   N =   W =
F =   O =   X =
G =   P =   Y =
H =   Q =   Z =
I =   R =

Do you know any good jokes?
—send them in and they might appear in XTB!

Do you have any questions?
...about anything you've read in XTB.
—send them in and we'll do our best to answer them.

Write to: XTB, The Good Book Company, Blenheim House, 1 Blenheim Epsom, Surrey, KT19 9AP, UK. **or email me:** alison@thegoodbook.c